BELLUM

BELLUM

TWO STATEMENTS ON THE
NATURE OF WAR

An Essay on War
written in 1545 by
ERASMUS

Fifty Etchings created
in 1923 & 1924 by
OTTO DIX

Imprint Society · BARRE · MASSACHUSETTS
MCMLXXII

CONTENTS

INTRODUCTION

B ELLUM *is as timely today as when it was written, the goal it proposes to humanity as desirable and, alas, as elusive. Peace, writes Erasmus, is nothing but 'love and amity subsisting between great numbers,' and war is 'hatred and enmity subsisting between great numbers.' He demonstrates the horrors and the folly of war more eloquently than has anyone before or since. No modern apologist has put forward arguments against war more persuasive than those of Erasmus, nor has anyone been able to devise practical means for its abolition any more than he could.*

It may be significant for our future that the 500th anniversary of the birth of Erasmus in 1969 aroused such intense interest internationally. We hope this reflects more than a desire to make a gesture of tribute to his genius, that it bespeaks a renewed awareness of the relevance of his thought and attitude of mind to our own problems, a sense that man holds the key to the solution of his difficulties if he will only learn to see clearly and act resolutely.

It seems to me that the spirit of Erasmus reveals a striking affinity with the distinctive national characteristics of the people of his country of origin. His influence on the national mood is still recognizable today, and in no field is it more perceptible than in the attitude of his fellow countrymen toward war. For this, as well as other reasons, I believe that were he alive today, Erasmus would feel more at home in the Netherlands than in any other country.

He would welcome the ecumenical spirit, for he always sought reconciliation. He would denounce fanaticism today as he did when he established the kinship of the True Christian and the Sage of Antiquity. He would oppose all crusades now as he did then, save that of the search for truth. Were he to write his Colloquies *in our time, he would no doubt again expose and deride what he felt to be aberrations of thought and practice, outworn habits of mind and the momentum of ideas no longer relevant to the problems of our age.*

I suspect that he would find in the Netherlands today a greater respect in theory and practice than elsewhere for the values which were dear to his heart. The role of letters, the 'bonae litterae,' the dignity of the book, the pursuit of true scholarship with integrity and without pedantry, the relationship between the graphic arts and literature—all these are today imbued with vitality and elegance in the country of his birth.

He would feel equally at home in the realm of ideas, in the instinctive aversion of his fellow countrymen to any justification of war, whatever the circumstances. He would find solace in the ardently proclaimed condemnation of racism and in their rejection of any form of nationalistic arrogance, let alone fanaticism, in international relations. He would find in his country a national springboard for the launching of ideas in support of European political unity, which he would advocate today as he strove to promote the cause of the spiritual unity of Europe in his time. He would find a sympathetic forum in which to marshal support for integration, for the abolition of barriers between peoples. He would identify himself with the aspirations of the great majority of his people toward the creation of European institutions in place of competition between national policies, and toward the abrogation of national sovereignty. He would find there an audience responsive to his attacks on arguments which seek to justify inertia on grounds of national interest.

The first publication of Bellum was as Adagium 3001, under the title Dulce bellum inexpertis, in the Froben edition of 1515. However, its origins go back to a letter which Erasmus wrote in March 1514 to Antonius van Bergen (abbot of the monastery of St. Bertin at St. Omer), brother of the benefactor of Erasmus, Hendrick van Bergen. It was first published as an independent work by Froben in April 1517.

WILLIAM ROYALL TYLER
United States Ambassador to the Netherlands
1965–1969

BELLUM

.

BELLUM

OF THERE IS in the affairs of mortal men any one thing which it is proper uniformly to explode; which it is incumbent on every man, by every lawful means, to avoid, to deprecate, to oppose, that one thing is doubtless war. There is nothing more unnaturally wicked, more productive of misery, more extensively destructive, more obstinate in mischief, more unworthy of man as formed by nature, much more of man Professing Christianity.

Yet, wonderful to relate, in these times, war is everywhere rashly, and on the slightest pretext, undertaken; cruelly and savagely conducted, not only by unbelievers, but by Christians; not only by laymen, but by priests and bishops; not only by the young and inexperienced, but even by men far advanced in life, who must have seen and felt its dreadful consequences; not only by the lower order, the rude rabble, fickle in their nature; but, above all, by princes, whose duty it is to compose the rash passions of the unthinking multitude by superior wisdom and the force of reason. Nor are there ever wanting men learned in the law, and even divines, who are ready to furnish firebrands for the nefarious work, and to fan the latent sparks into a flame.

Whence it happens, that WAR is now considered so much a thing of course, that the wonder is, how any man can disapprove of it; so much *sanctioned by authority* and custom, that it is deemed impious, I had almost said heretical, to have borne testimony against a practice in its principle most profligate, and in its effects pregnant with every kind of calamity.

How much more justly might it be matter of wonder, what evil genius, what accursed fiend, what hell-born fury first suggested to the mind of man, a propensity so brutal, such as instigates a gentle animal, formed by nature for peace and good will, formed to promote the welfare of all around him, to rush with mad ferocity on the destruction of himself and his fellow creatures!

Still more wonderful will this appear, if, laying aside all vulgar prejudices, and accurately examining the real nature of things, we contemplate with the eyes of philosophy, the portrait of man on one side, and on the other, the picture of war!

In the first place then, if any one considers a moment the organization and external figure of the body, will he not instantly perceive, that nature, or rather the God of Nature, created the human animal not for war, but for love and friendship; not for mutual destruction, but for mutual service and safety; not to commit injuries, but for acts of reciprocal beneficence.

To all other animals, nature, or the God of Nature, has given appropriate weapons of offence. The inborn violence of the bull is seconded by weapons of pointed horn; the rage of the lion with claws. On the wild boar are fixed terrible tusks. The elephant, in addition to the toughness of his hide and his enormous size, is defended with a proboscis. The crocodile is covered with scales as with a coat of mail. Fins serve the dolphin for arms; quills the porcupine; prickles the thornback; and the gallant chanticleer, in the farm-yard, crows defiance, conscious of his spur. Some are furnished with shells, some with hides, and others with external teguments, resembling, in strength and thickness, the rind of a tree. Nature has consulted the safety of some of her creatures, as of the dove, by velocity of motion. To others she has given venom as a substitute for a weapon; and added a hideous shape, eyes that beam terror, and a hissing noise. She has also given them antipathies and discordant dispositions corresponding with this exterior, that they might wage an offensive or defensive war with animals of a different species.

But man she brought into the world naked from his mother's womb, weak, tender, unarmed; his flesh of the softest texture, his skin smooth and delicate, and susceptible of the slightest injury. There is nothing observable in his limbs adapted to fighting, or to violence; not to mention that other animals are no sooner brought forth, than they are sufficient of themselves to support the life they have received; but man alone, for a long period, totally depends on extraneous assistance. Unable either to speak, or walk, or help himself to food, he can only implore relief by tears and wailing; so that from this circumstance alone might be collected, that man is an animal born for that love and friendship which is formed and cemented by the mutual interchange of benevolent offices. Moreover, Nature evidently intended that man should consider himself indebted for the boon of life, not so much to herself as to the kindness of his fellow man; that he might perceive himself designed for social affections, and the attachments of friendship and love. Then she gave him a countenance, not frightful and forbidding, but mild and placid, intimating by external signs the benignity of his disposition. She gave him eyes full of affectionate expression, the indexes of a mind delighting in social sympathy. She gave him arms to embrace his fellow-creatures. She gave him lips to express an union of heart and soul. She gave him alone the power of laughing; a mark of the joy, of which he is susceptible. She gave him alone tears, the symbol of clemency and compassion. She gave him also a voice; not a menacing and frightful yell, but bland, soothing, and friendly. Not satisfied with these marks of her peculiar favour, she bestowed on him alone the use of speech and reason; a gift which tends more than any other to conciliate and cherish benevolence, and a desire of rendering mutual services; so that nothing among human creatures might be done by violence. She implanted in man a hatred of solitude, and a love of company. She sowed in his heart the seeds of every benevolent affection; and thus rendered what is most salutary, at the same time most agreeable. For what is more agreeable than a friend? what so necessary? Indeed if it were possible to conduct life conveniently without mutual intercourse, yet nothing could be pleasant without a companion, unless man should have divested himself of humanity, and degenerated to the rank of a wild beast. Nature has also added a love of learning, an ardent desire of knowledge; a circumstance which at once contributes in the highest degree to distinguish man from the ferocity of inferior animals, and to endear him cordially to his fellow-creature: for neither the relationship of affinity nor of consanguinity binds congenial spirits with closer or firmer bands, than an union in one common pursuit of liberal knowledge and intellectual improvement. Add to all this, that she has distributed to every mortal, endowments both of mind and body, with such admirable variety, that every man finds in every other man, something to love and to admire for its beauty and excellence, or something to seek after and embrace for its use and necessity. Lastly, kind Providence has given to man a spark of the divine mind, which stimulates him, without any hope of reward, and of his own free will, to do good to all: for of God, this is the most natural and appropriate attribute, to consult the good of all by disinterested beneficence. If it were not so, how happens it that we feel an exquisite delight, when we find that any man has been preserved from danger, injury, or destruction, by our offices or intervention? How happens it that we love a man the better, because we have done him a service?

It seems as if God has placed man in this world, a representative of himself, a kind of terrestrial deity, to make provision for the general welfare. Of this the very brutes seem sensible, since we see not only tame animals, but leopards and lions, and, if there be any more fierce than they, flying for refuge, in extreme danger, to man. This is the last asylum, the most inviolable sanctuary, the anchor of hope in distress to every inferior creature.

Such is the true portrait of man, however faintly and imperfectly delineated. It remains that I compare it, as I proposed, with the picture of war; and see how the two tablets accord, when hung up together and contrasted.

Now then view, with the eyes of your imagination, savage troops of men, horrible in their very visages and voices; men, clad in steel, drawn up on every side in battle array, armed with weapons, frightful in their crash and their very glitter; mark the horrid murmur of the confused multitude, their threatening eye-balls, the harsh jarring din of drums and clarions, the terrific sound of the trumpet, the thunder of the cannon, a noise not less formidable than the real thunder of heaven, and more hurtful; a mad shout like that of the shrieks of bedlamites, a furious onset, a cruel butchering of each other!—See the slaughtered and the slaughtering!—heaps of dead bodies, fields flowing with blood, rivers reddened with human gore!—It sometimes happens that a brother falls by the hand of a brother, a kinsman upon his nearest kindred, a friend upon his friend, who, while both are actuated by this fit of insanity, plunges the sword into the heart of one by whom he was never offended, not even by a word of his mouth!—So deep is the tragedy, that the bosom shudders even at the feeble description of it, and the hand of humanity drops the pencil while it paints the scene.

In the mean time I pass over, as comparatively trifling, the corn-fields trodden down, peaceful cottages and rural mansions burnt to the ground, villages and towns reduced to ashes, the cattle driven from their pasture, innocent women violated, old men dragged into captivity, churches defaced and demolished, every thing laid waste, a prey to robbery, plunder, and violence!

Not to mention the consequences which ensue to the people after a war, even the most fortunate in its event, and the justest in its principle: the poor, the unoffending common people, robbed of their little hard-earned property: the great, laden with taxes: old people bereaved of their children; more cruelly killed by the murder of their offspring than by the sword; happier if the enemy had deprived them of the sense of their misfortune, and life itself, at the same moment: women far advanced in age, left destitute, and more cruelly put to death, than if they had died at once by the point of the bayonet; widowed mothers, orphan children, houses of mourning; and families, that once knew better days, reduced to extreme penury.

Why need I dwell on the evils which morals sustain by war, when every one knows, that from war proceeds at once every kind of evil which disturbs and destroys the happiness of human life?

Hence is derived a contempt of piety, a neglect of law, a general corruption of principle, which hesitates at no villainy. From this source rushes on society a torrent of thieves, robbers, sacrilegists, murderers; and, what is the greatest misfortune of all, this destructive pestilence confines not itself within its own boundaries; but, originating in one corner of the world, spreads its contagious virulence, not only over the neighbouring states, but draws the most remote regions, either by subsidies, by marriages among princes, or by political alliances, into the common tumult, the general whirlpool of mischief and confusion. One war sows the seeds of another. From a pretended war, arises a real one; from an inconsiderable skirmish, hostilities of most important consequence; nor is it uncommon, in the case of war, to find the old fable of the Lernæan Lake, or the Hydra realized. For this reason, I suppose, the ancient poets (who penetrated into the nature of things with wonderful sagacity, and shadowed them out with the aptest fictions) handed down by tradition, that war originated from hell, that it was brought thence by the assistance of Furies, and that only the most furious of the Furies, Alecto, was fit for the infernal office. The most pestilent of them all was selected for it.

As the poets describe her, she is armed with snakes without number, and blows her blast in the trumpet of hell. Pan fills all the space around her with mad uproar. Bellona, in frantic mood, shakes her scourge. And the unnatural, impious Fury, breaking every bond asunder, flies abroad all horrible to behold, with a visage besmeared with gore!

Even the grammarians, with all their trifling ingenuity, observing the deformity of war, say, that bellum, the Latin word for war, which signifies also the beautiful, or comely, was so called by the rhetorical figure Contradiction, because it has nothing in it either good or beautiful; and that bellum is called bellum, by the same figure as the furies are called Eumenides. Other etymologists, with more judgment, derive bellum from bellua, a beast, because it ought to be more characteristic of beasts than of men, to meet for no other purpose than mutual destruction.

But to me it appears to deserve a worse epithet than brutal; it is more than brutal, when men engage in the conflict of arms; ministers of death to men! Most of the brutes live in concord with their own kind, move together in flocks, and defend each other by mutual assistance. Indeed all kinds of brutes are not inclined to fight even their enemies. There are harmless ones like the hare. It is only the fiercest, such as lions, wolves, and tigers, that fight at all. A dog will not devour his own species; lions, with all their fierceness, are quiet among themselves; dragons are said to live in peace with dragons; and even venomous creatures live with one another in perfect harmony.—But to man, no wild beast is more destructive than his fellow man.

Again; when the brutes fight, they fight with the weapons which nature gave them; we arm ourselves for mutual slaughter, with weapons which nature never thought of, but which were invented by the contrivance of some accursed fiend, the enemy of human nature, that man might become the destroyer of man. Neither do the beasts break out in hostile rage for trifling causes; but either when hunger drives them to madness, or when they find themselves attacked, or when they are alarmed for the safety of their young. We, good Heaven! on frivolous pretences, what tragedies do we act on the theatre of war! Under colour of some obsolete and disputable claim to territory; in a childish passion for a mistress; for causes even more ridiculous than these, we kindle the flames of war. Among the beasts, the combat is for the most part only one against one, and for a very short space. And though the contest should be bloody, yet when one of them has received a wound, it is all over. Whoever heard (what is common among men in one campaign) that a hundred thousand beasts had fallen in battle by mutual butchery? Besides, as beasts have a natural hatred to some of a different kind, so are they united to others of a different kind, in a sincere and inviolable alliance. But man with man, and any man with any man, can find an everlasting cause for contest, and become, what they call, natural enemies; nor is any agreement or truce found sufficiently obligatory to bind man from attempting, on the appearance of the slightest pretexts, to commence hostilities after the most solemn convention. So true it is, that whatever has deviated from its own nature into evil, is apt to degenerate to a more depraved state, than if its nature had been originally formed with inbred malignity.

Do you wish to form a lively idea, however imperfect, of the ugliness and the brutality of war, (for we are speaking of its brutality,) and how unworthy it is of a rational creature? Have you ever seen a battle between a lion and a bear? What distortion, what roaring, what howling, what fierceness, what bloodshed! The spectator of a fray, in which mere brutes like these are fighting, though he stands in a place of safety, cannot help shuddering at a sight so bloody. But how much more shocking a spectacle to see man conflicting with man, armed from head to foot with a variety of artificial weapons! Who could believe that creatures so engaged were men, if the frequency of the sight had not blunted its effect on our feelings, and prevented surprise? Their eyes flashing, their cheeks pale, their very gait and mien expressive of fury; gnashing their teeth, shouting like madmen, the whole man transformed to steel; their arms clanging horribly, while the cannon's mouth thunders and lightens around them. It would really be less savage, if man destroyed and devoured man for the sake of necessary food, or drank blood through lack of beverage. Some, indeed, (men in form) have come to such a pitch as to do this from rancour and wanton cruelty, for which expediency or even necessity could furnish only a poor excuse. More cruel still, they fight on some occasions with weapons dipt in poison, and engines invented in Tartarus, for wholesale havoc at a single stroke.

You now see not a single trace of man, that social creature, whose portrait we lately delineated. Do you think Nature would recognize the work of her own hand—the image of God? And if any one were to assure her that it was so, would she not break out into execrations at the flagitious actions of her favourite creature? Would she not say, when she saw man thus armed against man, 'What new sight do I behold? Hell itself must have produced this portentous spectacle. There are, who call me a stepmother, because in the multiplicity of my works I have produced some that are venomous, (though even they are convertible to the use of man,) and because I created some, among the variety of animals, wild and fierce; though there is not one so wild and so fierce, but he may be tamed by good management and good usage. Lions have grown gentle, serpents have grown innoxious under the care of man. Who is this then, worse than a stepmother, who has brought forth a non-descript brute, the plague of the whole creation? I, indeed, made one animal, like this, in external appearance; but with kind propensities, all placid, friendly, beneficent. How comes it to pass, that he has degenerated to a beast, such as I now behold, still in the same human shape? I recognize no vestiage of man, as I created him. What Dæmon has marred the work of my hands? What Sorceress, by her enchantments, has discharged from the human figure, the human mind, and supplied its place with the heart of a brute? What Circe has transformed the man that I made into a beast? I would bid this wretched creature behold himself in a mirror, if his eyes were capable of seeing himself, when his mind is no more. Nevertheless, thou depraved animal, look at thyself, if thou canst; reflect on thyself, thou frantic warrior, if by any means thou mayest recover thy lost reason, and be restored to thy pristine nature. Take the looking-glass, and inspect it. How came that threatening crest of plumes upon thy head? Did I give thee feathers! Whence that shining helmet? Whence those sharp points, which appear like horns of steel? Whence are thy hands and arms furnished with sharp prickles? Whence those scales, like the scales of fish, upon thy body? Whence those brazen teeth? Whence those plates of brass all over thee? Whence those deadly weapons of offence? Whence that voice, uttering sounds of rage more horrible than the inarticulate noise of the wild beasts? Whence the whole form of thy countenance and person distorted by furious passions, more than brutal? Whence that thunder and lightning which I perceive around thee, at once more frightful than the thunder of heaven, and more destructive to man? I formed thee an animal a little lower than the angels, a partaker of divinity; how camest thou to think of transforming thyself into a beast so savage, that no beast hereafter can be deemed a beast, if it be compared with man, originally the image of God, the Lord of the creation?'

Such, and much more, would, I think, be the outcry of indignant nature, the architect of all things, viewing man transformed to a warrior.

Now, since man was so made by nature, as I have above shown him to have been, and since war is that which we too often feel it to be, it seems matter of infinite astonishment, what dæmon of mischief, what distemperature, or what fortuitous circumstances, could put it into the heart of man to plunge the deadly steel into the bosom of his fellow-creature.

What is war but murder and theft, committed by great numbers on great numbers? the greatness of numbers not only not extenuating its malignity, but rendering it the more wicked, in proportion as it is thus more extended, in its effects and its influence.

But all this is laughed at as the dream of men unacquainted with the world, by the stupid, ignorant, unfeeling grandees of our time, who, though they possess nothing of man but the form, yet seem to themselves little less than earthly divinities.

Man has arrived at such a degree of insanity, that war seems to be the grand business of human life. We are always at war, either in preparation, or in action. Nation rises against nation; and, what the heathens would have reprobated as unnatural, relatives against their nearest kindred, brother against brother, son against father!—more atrocious still!—a Christian against a man! and, worst of all, a Christian against a Christian! And such is the blindness of human nature, that nobody feels astonishment at all this, nobody expresses detestation. There are thousands and tens of thousands ready to applaud it all, to extol it to the skies, to call transactions truly hellish, a holy war. There are many who spirit up princes to war, mad enough as they usually are of themselves; yet are there many who are always adding fuel to their fire. One man mounts the pulpit, and promises remission of sins to all who will fight under the banners of his prince. Another exclaims, 'O invincible prince! only keep your mind favourable to the cause of religion, and God will fight (his own creatures) for you.' A third promises certain victory, perverting the words of the prophetical psalmist to the wicked and unnatural purposes of war. 'Thou shalt not be afraid for the terror by night, nor for the arrow that flieth by day. A thousand shall fall at thy side, and ten thousand at thy right hand; but it shall not come nigh thee.' Psalm xci.

The whole of this mystical psalm is wrested to signify something in favour of the most profane of all profane things, and to second the interested views of this or that earthly potentate. Both parties find such passages in the prophets or the psalmist on their own side; and such interpreters of the prophets fail not to find their admirers, their applauders, and their followers.

Such warlike sermons have we heard from the mouths of grave divines, and even of bishops. These men are, in fact warriors; they help on the cause. Decrepit as they are in person, they fight from the pulpit the battles of the prince, who, perhaps, raised them to their eminence. Priests fight, in fact, when they set others on to fight; even monks fight, and, in a business truly diabolical, dare to use the name and authority of Jesus Christ.

Thus two armies shall meet in the field, both bearing before them the standard of the cross, which alone might suggest to their minds, how the followers of Christ are to carry on their warfare, and to gain their victory.

St. Paul expresses his indignation, that there should be even a hostile controversy or dispute among Christians; he rather disapproves even litigation before a Judge and Jury. What would he have said, if he had seen us waging war all over the world; waging war on the most trifling causes, with more ferocity than any of the heathens, with more cruelty than any savages; led on, exhorted, assisted by those who represent a Pontiff professing to be pacific, and to cement all Christendom under his influence; and who salute the people committed to their charge with the phrase, 'peace be unto you!'

I am well aware what a clamour those persons will raise against me who reap a harvest from public calamity. 'We engage in war,' they always say, 'with reluctance, provoked by the aggression and the injuries of the enemy. We are only prosecuting our own rights. Whatever evil attends war, let those be responsible for it who furnished the occasion of this war, a war to us just and necessary.'

But if they would hold their vociferous tongues a little while, I would show, in a proper place, the futility of their pretences, and take off the varnish with which they endeavour to disguise their mischievous iniquity.

As I just now drew the portrait of man and the picture of war, and compared one with the other, that is, compared an animal the mildest in his nature, with an institution of the most barbarous kind; and as I did this that war might appear, on the contrast, in its own black colours; so now it is my intention to compare war with peace; to compare a state most pregnant with misery, and most wicked in its origin, with a state profuse of blessings, and contributing, in the highest degree, to the happiness of human nature; it will then appear to be downright insanity to go in search of war with so much disturbance, so much labour, so great profusion of blood and treasure, and at such a hazard after all, when with little labour, less expense, no bloodshed, and no risque, peace might be preserved inviolate.

Now amidst all the good this world affords, what is more delightful to the heart of man, what more beneficial to society, than love and amity? Nothing, surely. Yet what is peace, but love and amity subsisting between great numbers? And, on the other hand, what is war, but hatred and enmity subsisting between great numbers? But it is the nature of all good, that the more it is extended, the greater the good becomes, the more benign its influence; therefore, if the amicable union of individuals is so sweet and so salutary, how much will the sum total of happiness be augmented, if kingdom with kingdom, and nation with nation, coalesce in this amicable union? On the other hand, it is the nature of all evil, that its malignity increases the more it is extended; and therefore, if it is wretched, if it is wicked, for one man to meet another with a sword pointed at his vitals, how much more wretched and more wicked, that thousands and tens of thousands should meet in the same manner? By union, little things are augmented to a respectable magnitude; by disunion, the greatest fall to insignificance and dissolution. Peace is, indeed, at once the mother and the nurse of all that is good for man: war, on a sudden, and at one stroke, overwhelms, extinguishes, abolishes, whatever is cheerful, whatever is happy and beautiful, and pours a foul torrent of disasters on the life of mortals. Peace shines upon human affairs like the vernal sun. The fields are cultivated, the gardens bloom, the cattle are fed upon a thousand hills, new buildings arise, ancient edifices are repaired, riches flow, pleasures smile, laws retain their vigour, the discipline of the police prevails, religion glows with ardour, justice bears sway, humanity and charity increase, arts and manufactures feel the genial warmth of encouragement, the gains of the poor are more plentiful, the opulence of the rich displays itself with additional splendour, liberal studies flourish, the young are well educated, the old enjoy their ease, marriages are happy, good men thrive, and the bad are kept under controul. But no sooner does the storm of war begin to lower, than what a deluge of miseries and misfortunes seizes, inundates, and overwhelms all things within the sphere of its action! The flocks are scattered, the harvest trampled, the husbandman butchered, villas and villages burnt, cities and states, that have been ages rising to their flourishing state, subverted by the fury of one tempest, the storm of war. So much easier is the task of doing harm than of doing good; of destroying than of building up! The earnings of honest industry, the wealth of quiet citizens are transferred to the pockets of execrable robbers and murderers. Private houses exhibit the dismal effects of fear, sorrow, and complaint; and all places resound with the voice of lamentation. The loom stands still; the trowel, the axe, and the hammer are silent; and the poor manufacturers must either starve, or have recourse to wicked practices for daily bread. The rich either deplore the diminution and loss of their property, or lie under terrible apprehension for what remains; in both circumstances rendered by war incapable of enjoying the common comforts of life. Marriages are few, or attended with distressful and fatal consequences. Matrons, deserted by their husbands, now forced to the wars, pine at home in childless solitude. The laws are compelled to silence, charity is laughed at, justice has no dwelling-place, and religion becomes an object of scorn, till no distinction is left between the sacred and the profane. Youth is corrupted by every species of vice; old men lament their longevity; and their grey hairs descend with sorrow to the grave. No honour is paid to learning, sciences, arts; the elegant pursuits of liberal and honourable minds. In a word, more misery is felt from war than the eloquence of any man, much more than mine, is able to describe: yet it might be born patiently, if war made us miserable only, and did not corrupt our morals, and involve us in guilt; if peace made us only happier, and not better: but the man who engages in war by choice, that man, whoever he is, is a wicked man: he sings against nature, against God, against man, and is guilty of the most aggravated and complicated impiety.

Too many, alas! are the evils by which miserable mortality is of necessity tormented, worn out, and at last overwhelmed. Two thousand years ago, no fewer than three hundred names of dangerous diseases, besides their various species and degrees, were discovered by the physicians: and every day, even now, new diseases arise. Old age itself is a disease, an incurable disease. We read of whole cities buried in ruins by earthquakes, or burnt to ashes by lightning, whole countries swallowed up in chasms occasioned by subterraneous convulsions; not to mention how many men are lost by casualties, which, by the frequency of their occurrence, cease to surprise; how many are drowned in seas and rivers; how many destroyed by poison, by falling, by other accidents; how many by intemperance in food, in drink, in sleep. The most trifling thing can deprive man of life. A grapestone in the throat, a hair, a bone of a fish, has brought many to an untimely grave. Sudden joy has been fatal: no wonder that grief has been so. Add to all this the plague, and pestilent, contagious fevers of various kinds, which frequently commit their ravages, without mercy or distinction, throughout a whole city or province. There is no quarter from which danger does not hang, as it were, by a hair over the life of man. Life itself, even if no accident shorten it, flies away with the swiftest velocity. Such and so great are the miseries of human life, that Homer did not hesitate to pronounce man, of all creatures, to whom the breath of life has been given, the most miserable. But these evils, as they cannot easily be shunned, and fall on our heads without any fault of our own, make us indeed wretched, but do not render us guilty.

Nevertheless, why should those who are obnoxious to so many calamities go voluntarily in quest of an adscititious evil, as if the measure of misery required to be full to the very brim, and to run over; in quest of an evil, not a common evil, but an evil, of all human evils, the worst and the foulest; so destructive an evil, that alone it exceeds them all in mischief; so abundant in misery, that it comprehends every kind of wretchedness within itself; so pestilential in its nature, that it loads men with guilt in proportion as it galls them with woe.

To these considerations add, that the advantages derived from peace diffuse themselves far and wide, and reach great numbers; while in war, if any thing turns out happily, (though, O my God, what can ever deserve the appellation of happy in war!) the advantage redounds only to a few, and those unworthy of reaping it. One man's safety is owing to the destruction of another; one man's prize derived from the plunder of another. The cause of rejoicings made by one side, is to the other a cause of mourning. Whatever is unfortunate in war, is severely so indeed; and whatever, on the contrary, is called good fortune, is a savage and a cruel good fortune, an ungenerous happiness deriving its existence from another's woe. Indeed, at the conclusion, it commonly happens, that both sides, the victorious and the vanquished, have cause to deplore. I know not whether any war ever succeeded so fortunately in all its events, but that the conqueror, if he had a heart to feel, or an understanding to judge, as he ought to do, repented that he ever engaged in it at all.

Therefore, since peace is confessedly of all things the best and the happiest, and war, on the contrary, appears to be attended with the greatest possible distress of every kind, and the blackest villainy of which human nature is capable, can we think those men of sound mind or honest hearts, who, when they might enjoy the blessings of peace with little trouble, merely by negociation, go out of their way, rush headlong into every difficulty and danger, to involve a whole people in the horrors of war?

How unpleasant, in the first place, to the unoffending people, is the first rumour of war? and in the next, how unpopular does it render the prince, when he is compelled to rob his own subjects by taxes upon taxes, and tribute upon tribute! How much trouble and anxiety in forming and preserving alliances! How much in engaging foreign troops, who are let out by their owners to fight for hire! How much expense, and at the same time solicitude, in fitting out fleets, in building or repairing forts, in manufacturing all kinds of camp equipage, in fabricating and transporting machines, armour, weapons, baggage, carriages, provisions! What infinite fatigue in fortifying towns, digging trenches, excavating mines, in keeping watch and ward, in exercising, reviewing, manœuvring, marching and countermarching! I say nothing of the constant state of fear and alarm, in which the people live: I say nothing of the real danger to which they are perpetually exposed. Such is the uncertainty of war, that what is there not to be feared in it? Who can enumerate the inconveniences and hardships which they who foolishly go to war, endure in a camp; deserving greater, because they voluntarily undergo all that they suffer! Food such as a hog would loath; beds which even a bug would disdain; little sleep, and that little at the will of another; a tent exposed to every bitter blast that blows, and often not even a tent to shelter their cold limbs from the wind and the weather! They must continue all night, as well as day, in the open air; they must lie on the ground; they must stand in their arms; they must bear hunger, cold, heat, dust, rain; they must be in a state of abject slavery to their leaders; even beaten with canes! There is, indeed, no kind of slavery on earth more unworthy man than the slavery of these poor wretches! After all these hardships, comes the dreadful signal for engagement! To death they must go! They must either slay without mercy, or fall without pity!

Such and so great are the evils which are submitted to, in order to accomplish an end, itself a greater evil than all that have preceded in preparation for it. We thus afflict ourselves for the noble end of enabling ourselves to afflict others. If we were to calculate the matter fairly, and form a just computation of the cost attending war, and that of procuring peace, we should find that peace might be purchased at a tenth part of the cares, labours, troubles, dangers, expenses, and blood, which it costs to carry on a war. You lead a vast multitude of men into danger of losing their lives, in order to demolish some great city; while the same labour and fatigue of these very men would build, without any danger, a more magnificent city than the city doomed to demolition. But the object is to do all possible injury to an enemy. A most inhuman object, let me tell you! And consider, whether you can hurt him essentially, without hurting, at the same time, and by the same means, your own people. It surely is to act like a madman to take to yourself so large a portion of certain evil, when it must ever be uncertain how the die of war may fall in the ultimate issue.

But grant that the heathens might be hurried into all this madness and folly by anger, by ambition, by avarice, by cruelty, or, which I am rather inclined to believe, by the furies sent from hell for that very purpose; yet how could it ever enter into our hearts, that a Christian should imbrue his hands in the blood of a Christian! If a brother murder his brother, the crime is called fratricide: but a Christian is more closely allied to a Christian as such, than a brother by the ties of consanguinity; unless the bonds of nature are stronger than the bonds of Christ, which Christians, consistently with their faith, cannot allow. How absurd then is it, that they should be constantly at war with each other; who form but one family, the church of Christ; who are members of the same body; who boast of the same head, even Jesus Christ; who have one Father in Heaven, common to them all; who grow in grace by the same spirit; who are initiated in the same common mysteries, and ultimately redeemed by identical Christian blood.

Where are there so many and so sacred obligations to perfect concord as in the Christian religion! Where so numerous exhortations to peace? One law Jesus Christ claimed as his own peculiar law, and it was the law of love, or charity. What practice among mankind violates this law so grossly as war? Christ salutes his votaries with the happy omen of peace. To his disciples he gives nothing but peace; he leaves them no other legacy but peace. In his holy prayers, the subject of his devout entreaty was principally, that, as he was one with the Father, so his disciples, that is to say, all Christians, might be one with him. This union is something more than peace, more than friendship, more than concord, it is an intimate communion with the divine nature.

Solomon was a type of Christ. But the word Solomon in Hebrew signifies the pacific. Solomon, on this account, because he was pacific, was chosen to build the temple. David, though endeared by some virtues, was rejected as a builder of the temple, because he had stained his hands in blood, because he was a sanguinary prince, because, in a word, he was a warrior. He was rejected for this, though the wars he carried on were against the wicked, and at the command of God; and though he, who afterwards abrogated, in great measure, the laws of Moses, had not yet taught mankind that they ought to love their enemies.

At the nativity of Jesus Christ, the angels sung not the glories of war, nor a song of triumph, but a hymn of peace. 'Glory to God in the highest; on earth, peace; good-will towards men.' The mystic poet and prophet fortold before his birth,

Factus est in pace locus ejus.—PSALM LXXVI. 2.

In the city of peace (Salem) he made his dwelling-place: there brake he the arrows of the bow, the shield, the sword, and the battle-axe.

He shall refrain the spirit of princes; he is terrible to the kings of the earth. Examine every part of his doctrine, you will find nothing that does not breathe peace, speak the language of love, and savour of charity: and as he knew that peace could not be preserved, unless those objects, for which the world contends with the sword's point, were considered as vile and contemptible, he ordered us to learn of him to be meek and lowly. He pronounced those happy who held riches, and the daughters of riches, pomp and pride, in no esteem; for these he calls the poor in spirit, and these he has blessed. He pronounced those happy, who despised the pleasures of the world; for he says, blessed are the mourners; even they who patiently suffered themselves to be extruded from their possessions, knowing that our place of residence on earth is a place of exile, and that our true country and our best riches are in heaven. He pronounced those happy who, while deserving well of all, should be evil-spoken of, and persecuted with ill-usage. He prohibited resistance of evil. In short, as the whole of his doctrine recommended forbearance and love, so his life taught nothing but mildness, gentleness, and kind affection. Such was his reign; thus did he wage war, thus he conquered, and thus he triumphed.

Nor do the apostles inculcate any other doctrine; they who had imbibed the purest spirit of Christ, and were filled with sacred draughts from the fountain head before it was polluted. What do all the epistles of St. Paul resound with but peace, but long-suffering, but charity? What does St. John speak of and repeat continually, but Christian love? What else St. Peter? What else all writers in the world who are truly Christian?

Whence then the tumults of war among the children of peace? Is it a mere fable, when Christ calls himself the vine, and his disciples the branches? Who can conceive a branch divided against a branch of the same tree? Or is it an unmeaning assertion, which St. Paul has repeatedly made, that the church is one body, united in its many members, and adhering to one head, Jesus Christ? Who ever beheld the eye contending with the hand, or the belly fighting against the foot?

In the whole universe, consisting of parts so discordant, there still continues a general harmony. In the animal body there is peace among all the members; and with whatever excellence one member is endowed, it confines not the benefit to itself, but communicates it to all. If any evil happen to one member, the whole body affords its assistance. Can then the mere animal connexion of nature in a material body, formed soon to perish, effect more in preserving harmony, than the union of the spirit in a mystical and immortal body? Is it without meaning that we pray, according to the command of Christ, thy will be done on earth as it is in heaven? In the kingdom of heaven there is perfect concord. But Christ intended that his church should be nothing less than a celestial community, a heaven upon earth; men who belong to it living, as much as possible, according to the model of the heavenly kingdom, hastening thither, and feeling and acknowledging their whole dependance upon it for present and future felicity.

Come then, and let us picture in imagination some stranger, just arrived at this world of ours, and desirous of knowing what is going on here: and when he has been informed of the various living creatures upon its surface, let him be told that there is one animal, wonderfully composed of two distinct parts; of a body which he possesses in common with the brutes; of a mind which bears a semblance of the divine mind, and is the image of the Creator; that he is so noble in his nature, that though here in a state of exile, yet has he dominion over all other animals; that feeling his celestial origin, he is always aspiring at heaven and immortality; that he is so dear to the eternal Deity, that, since he was unable, either by the powers of nature, or the deductions of philosophy, to reach the excellence at which he aspired, the eternal Deity delegated his own Son to bring to him from heaven a new doctrine. Then, after the stranger should have heard the whole life of Christ, and become perfectly acquainted with his laws and precepts, let us suppose him to ascend some lofty pinnacle, whence he might see with his own eyes the things which he had heard by report concerning this noble animal, rational, Christian, immortal man.

When he should have seen all other animals living at peace with their own kind, guided by the laws of nature, and desiring nothing but what nature taught them to desire: but at the same time observed, that there was one animal, and one alone, trafficing dishonestly, intriguing treacherously, quarrelling and waging war with its own kind, would he not be apt to suspect any of the other animals to be man, of whom he had heard so much, rather than that two-legged creature which is really man, thus perverted, as he would appear, from the state in which God made, and to which Christ came to restore him? But suppose the stranger informed by some guide, that this animal is really man, he would next look about to find in what place these Christian animals have fixed their abode, and where, following their divine Teacher, they are now exhibiting the model of an angelic community. Would he not imagine that Christians must choose their residence any where, rather than in countries, where he sees so much superfluous opulence, luxury, lust, pride, indolence, tyranny, ambition, fraud, envy, anger, discord, quarrels, fightings, battles, wars, tumults, in a word, a more abominable sink of all that Christ condemns, than is to be found among the Turks and the Saracens?

The question then naturally arises, how this pestilence of war first insinuated itself among a Christian people? This evil, like most other evils, made its way by little and little among those who were off their guard. All evil, indeed, either gradually and invisibly creeps into the life of man, or forces its way under the disguise of seeming good.

In the church militant, learning was the first auxiliary engaged to fight for religion. It was a desirable ally, in a contest with heretics, who come to the combat armed with the literature of philosophers, poets, and orators. Indeed, in the earliest ages of Christianity, the professors of it did not arm themselves for defence even with learning, but relied on those converts, who brought the profane knowledge which they had acquired before they had gained a knowledge of Christ, to the aid of piety and the Christian cause. Next eloquence, which had rather been concealed at first than despised, came openly forward, and was approved as an auxiliary. In process of time, under the pretence of defeating heretics, the vain ambition of ostentatious disputation crept into the church, and became its bane. The matter proceeded so far, that Aristotle was admitted into the midst of the Christian sanctuary; and admitted so implicitly, that his authority carried with it a sanction paramount to the authority of Christ: for if Christ had said any thing that did not perfectly square with the received modes of conducting life, it was lawful to turn it a little aside by an ingenious comment: but the man did not dare to show his head, who had presumed to oppose, in the slightest manner, the oracular edicts of the Stagirite. From him we learned, that the happiness of man could not be complete without the goods of the body and of fortune. From him we learned, that a state could not flourish in which was a Christian equality. Every one of his dogmas we endeavoured to incorporate with the doctrine of Christ, which is much the same as to attempt the commixture of water and fire. We admitted something also from the Roman laws, on account of the apparent equity which they displayed; and that they might agree the better, we forced by violence, as far as we could, the doctrine of the gospel into a conformity with these laws. But these laws permit us to repel force by force; they allow every one to litigate; they approve of all traffic; they admit of usury, provided it is moderate; they extol war as glorious, provided it is just; and they define that war to be a just war which is declared so by any prince, though the prince be either a child or a fool. Lastly; the whole doctrine of Christ was by this time so adulterated by the learning of heathen logicians, sophists, mathematicians, orators, poets, philosophers, and lawyers, that the greatest portion of life was necessarily consumed before time could be found to examine the mysterious learning of the gospel; to which, though men came at last, they could not but come tinged or prejudiced with so many worldly opinions, that the laws and precepts of Christ either gave offence, or were made to bend to the dogmas preconceived in the schools of heathenism: and this was so far from being disapproved, that it was a crime for a man to speak of evangelical knowledge, who had not plunged, as the phrase is, over head and ears in the nugatory and sophistical nonsense of Aristotle; as if the doctrine of Christ were of that kind which could not be adapted to the lowest degrees of intellect or attainments, or could by any means coalesce with the vain wisdom of mere human philosophy.

After this, Christians admitted among them something of honourable distinctions, offered, indeed, at first as a voluntary tribute, but soon demanded as a debt to merit. So far there appeared nothing unreasonable. The next step was to admit riches; first to be distributed for the relief of the poor, and then for their own private use; and why not? since that methodical arrangement of duties was soon learnt, which suggested that charity begins at home, and that every man is to himself the nearest and dearest neighbour. Nor was a pretext wanting for this deviation from Christian disinterestedness. It was but natural to provide for children, and no more than right to look forward to approaching old age. Why, indeed, should any man, said they, refuse riches if they fall to him honestly? By these gradations, things came to such a pass, that he at last was thought the best man who was the richest man; nor at any period was greater respect paid to riches among the heathens than at this day among Christians. For what is there, either sacred or profane, which is not governed among them by the despotism of money?

To all these extraneous embellishments or fancied improvements of original Christianity, it was now conceived, that it might not be amiss to add a little power. This also was admitted, but with an apparent moderation. In short, it was admitted upon these terms, that Christians, satisfied with the title and claim to power, should leave the thing itself to others administration. At length, and by insensible degrees, the matter proceeded so far, that a bishop could not believe himself a bishop in earnest, unless he possessed a little particle of worldly power. And the inferior clergy, if beneficed, thought themselves dishonoured, if, with all their holiness, they could not possess at least as much weight and influence as the profane grandees who lorded it over the earth with ungodly rule.

In the ultimate stage of the progress, Christians put a bold face upon the matter, banished every childish blush, and broke down every bar of modesty and moderation. Whatever at any time there has been of avarice, whatever of ambition, whatever of luxury, whatever of pomp and pride, whatever of despotism among the poor heathens; the whole of it, however enormous, the Christians now imitated, equalled, and surpassed.

But to wave more trifling articles, did the heathens, at any period of their history, carry on war either so continually, or more cruelly, than it has been carried on among Christians? How many pitiless storms of war, how many treaties broken, how much slaughter and devastation have we seen only within the few years just elapsed? What nation in all Christendom which has not drawn the sword on its neighbour? Christians, after all, revile unbelievers; as if there could be a more pleasing and diverting spectacle to unbelievers, than that which we Christians every day exhibit to them by our mutual slaughter. Xerxes was stark mad when he led on that immense multitude to invade Greece. Could he be otherwise than mad, who sent letters menacing Mount Athos with vengeance, if it should not give way and yield him a passage; who ordered the Hellespont to be whipped with scourges, because it did not smooth its waters to facilitate the transportation of his vessels? Alexander the Great was stark mad: no man ever denied it: he thought himself a demi-god, and wished for more worlds to conquer; so ardently did he burn with a feverish thirst for glory. And yet these two persons, whom Seneca does not hesitate to call robbers as well as madmen, conducted war with more humanity than we; conducted war with more good faith; they fought not with weapons so unnaturally, so ingeniously cruel, nor with similar contrivances for mischief, nor on so frivolous pretences, as we, the followers of Jesus Christ. If you review the history of the heathen nations, how many chieftains will you find, who declined engaging in war, by every studied means of reconciliation; who chose rather to win over an enemy by kindness, than to subdue him by arms? Some even preferred the cession of a principality to running the hazard of war. We, Pseudo-Christians, or Christians only in name, eagerly seize every trifle that can possibly serve as an occasion of war. The heathen warriors, before they came to blows, had recourse to conference. Among the Romans, after every expedient had been tried in vain to preserve peace, a herald was dispatched with many formalities; certain preliminary ceremonies were gone through; and delays thus industriously contrived, to temper the fury of the first onset. And even after this prelude was finished, no soldier durst begin the battle till the signal was given; and the signal was contrived to be given in such a manner, that no one could know the exact time of it, but all waited for it patiently; nor, after the signal was once heard, was it lawful for any man to attack or strike the enemy, who had not taken the military oath. The elder Cato actually sent orders to his own son, who was loitering in the camp, but had not taken the oath, to return to Rome; or, if he chose rather to remain with the army, to ask permission of the general to engage the enemy. As the signal for engagement did not give liberty to fight to any but those who had taken the oath; so, the signal once sounded for retreat immediately deprived every soldier of the liberty to kill a single individual in the enemy's army. The great Cyrus publicly honoured with his praise, a private soldier, who though he had lifted up his sword to cut down one of the enemy, instantly withdrew it and spared the foe, on hearing the signal for cessation of battle. This was so ordered by the heathens, in their wars, that no man might imagine himself at liberty to slay a fellow-creature, unless compelled by unavoidable necessity.

Now, among Christians, the man is esteemed a brave fellow, who, meeting one of the nation with whom he is at war in a wood, unarmed, but laden with money; not intending to fight, but endeavouring to make his escape, lest he should be forced to fight; slays him, robs him when slain, and buries him when robbed. Those also are called soldiers, who, incited with the hope of a little paltry gain, eagerly hasten as volunteers to the battle, ready to bear arms on either side, even against their own kindred and their own prince. Wretches like these, when they return home from such engagements, presume to relate their exploits as soldiers; nor are punished as they ought to be, like robbers, traitors, and deserters. Every one holds the common hangman in abhorrence, though hired to do his work, though he only puts to death those who are found guilty, and condemned by the laws of his country; while, at the same time, men who, forsaking their parents, their wives, and their children, rush as volunteers or privateers into the war, not hired, but ambitious to be hired, for the unnatural work of human butchery, shall be received, when they return home, with a heartier welcome than if they had never gone to rob and murder. By such exploits they imagine that they acquire something of nobility. A man is counted infamous who steals a coat; but if the same man goes to the wars, and, after shedding blood, returns from the battle, laden with the property of a great number of innocent men, he is ranked among honest and reputable members of society: and any one among the common soldiers, who has behaved himself with remarkable ferocity, is judged worthy of being made a petty officer in the next war. If therefore we duly consider the humane discipline of the ancient warriors in heathen nations, the wars of Christians will appear, on comparison, to be merely systems of plunder.

And if you contrast Christian monarchs with heathen monarchs in their conduct of war, in how much worse a light will the Christians appear? The kings of the heathens sought not gain, but glory; they took delight in promoting the prosperity of the provinces which they subdued in war; barbarous nations, who lived like the brutes, without letters and without laws, they polished and refined by the arts of civilization; they adorned uncultivated regions by building cities and towns in them; whatever they found unprotected, they fortified; they built bridges, they embanked rivers, they drained swamps, they improved human life, they facilitated and sweetened human intercourse, by a thousand similar accommodations; so that it became in those days of generous heroism, an advantage to have been conquered. How many things are handed down to us by tradition, which they said wisely, or acted humanely and temperately, even in the midst of war. But the military transactions of Christians are too offensive and atrocious to bear particular enumeration. Upon the whole, whatever was the worst part of the conduct of heathens in war, that alone we closely imitate, in that alone we exceed them.

It may now be worth while to observe in what manner Christians defend the madness of war.

If, say they, war had been absolutely unlawful, God would not have excited the Jews to wage war against their enemies. I hear the argument, and observe upon it, that the objector should in justice add, that the Jews scarcely ever waged war, as the Christians do, against each other, but against aliens and infidels. We Christians draw the sword against Christians. To them, a difference in religion, and the worship of strange gods, was the source of contest. We are urged to war either by childish anger, or a hunger and thirst for riches and glory, and oftentimes merely for base and filthy lucre. They fought at the express command of God; we at the command of our own passions. But if we are so fond of the Jewish model as to make their going to war a precedent for us, why do we not, at the same time, adopt their practice of circumcision? Why not sacrifice cattle? Why not abstain from swine's flesh? Why not admit polygamy? Since we execrate these practices, why do we pitch upon their warlike actions as the only model for our imitation? Why, lastly, do we follow the letter which killeth, and neglect the spirit of their institutions? To the Jews, war was permitted, for the same reason as divorce, because of the hardness of their hearts.

But since the time that Jesus Christ said, put up thy sword into its scabbard, Christians ought not to go to war; unless it be in that most honourable warfare, with the vilest enemies of the Church, the inordinate love of money, anger, ambition, and the fear of death. These are our Philistines, these our Nabuchodonosors, these our Moabites and Ammonites, with whom we ought never to make a truce: with these we must engage without intermission, till the enemy being utterly extirpated, peace may be firmly established. Unless we subdue such enemies as these, we can neither have peace with ourselves, nor peace with any one else. This is the only war which tends to produce a real and lasting peace. He who shall have once conquered foes like these, will never wish to wage war with any mortal man upon the face of that earth, on which God placed all men to live, to let live, and to enjoy the life he gave.

I lay no stress on the opinion of those who interpret the two swords given to Peter to mean two powers, the civil and ecclesiastical, claimed by the successors of Peter; since Christ suffered Peter himself to fall into an error in this matter, on purpose that, when he was ordered to put up his sword, it might remain no longer a doubt, that war was prohibited; which, before that order, had been considered as allowable. But Peter, they allege, did actually use his sword. It is true he did; but while he was still a Jew, and had not yet received the genuine spirit of Christianity. He used his sword, not in support of any disputable claim to property; not to defend goods, chattels, lands, and estates, as we do; nor yet for his own life, but for the life of his Lord and Master. Let it also be remembered, that he who used the sword in defence of his Master, very soon after denied and renounced that Master. If Peter is to be our model, and if we are so much pleased with the example of Peter fighting for Christ, we may probably approve also the example of Peter denying Christ.

Peter, in using his sword, only made a slip in consequence of the impulse of a sudden passion, yet he was reprimanded. But if Christ approved this mode of defence, as some most absurdly infer from this transaction, how happens it that the uniform tenor of his whole life and doctrine teaches nothing else but forbearance? Why, when he commissioned his disciples, did he expose them to the despots of the world, armed only with a walking-stick and a wallet—a staff and a scrip? If by that sword, which Christ ordered them, after selling every thing else, to buy, is meant a moderate defence against persecution, as some men not only ignorantly but wickedly interpret it, how came it to pass that the martyrs never used it?

Here it is usual to bring forward the Rabbinical limitations, and to say, that it is lawful for a hired soldier to fight, just as it is for a butcher to practise his trade for a livelihood: since the one has served an apprenticeship to the art of killing sheep and oxen, and the other to the art of killing men, both may equally follow their trade in perfect consistence with the character of good and worthy members of society, provided always that the war be just and necessary. And their definition of a just and necessary war is as follows:—That is a just and necessary war which, whatsoever it be, howsoever it originates, on whomsoever it is waged, any prince whatever may have thought proper to declare. Priests may not indeed actually brandish the sword of war, but they may be present at, preside over, and superintend by their counsels, all its operations. They would not, indeed, for the world go to war from motives of revenge, but solely from a love of justice, and a desire to promote a righteous cause: but what man alive is there who does not think, or at least maintain, that his own cause is a righteous cause?

The world had its own laws and its own established practices before the Gospel appeared; it punished with death, it waged war, it heaped up pelf, both into the public treasury and into the private coffer; it wanted not to be taught what it already knew and practised. Our Lord did not come to tell the world what enormity was permitted, how far we might deviate from the laws of rectitude, but to shew us the point of perfection at which we were to aim with the utmost of our ability.

But they urge, that the laws of nature, the laws of society, and the laws of custom and usage, conspire in dictating the propriety of repelling force by force, and defending life—and money too, which, as Hesiod says, is to some persons as dear as life. So much I allow. But Gospel grace, of more force than all these laws, declares, in decisive words, that those who revile us, we must not revile again; that we must do good to them who use us ill; that to those who take a part of our possessions, we should give up the whole; and that we should also pray for them who design to take away our lives. All this, they tell us, had a particular reference to the apostles; but I contend that it also refers to all Christian people, to the whole body, which should be entire and perfect, though one member may have been formerly distinguished by some particular pre-eminence. The doctrine of Christ can, indeed, have no reference to them, who do not expect their reward with Christ. Let those draw swords for money, for land, and for power, who laugh at Christ's saying, that the poor in spirit were the happy men; that is, that those were the truly rich, who desired none of this world's riches or honours. They who place the chief good in things like these, fight for their lives; but then they are of that description of persons, who are not sensible that this life is a kind of death, and that to the godly there is provided a treasure of Heaven, a happy immortality.

They object to us, that there have been Roman Pontiffs who authorized war, and took an active part in it. They farther object those opinions or decrees of the fathers, in which war seems to be approved. Of this sort there are some; but they are only among the later writers, who appeared when the true spirit of Christianity began to languish; and they are very few; while, on the other hand, there are innumerable ones among writers of acknowledged sanctity, which absolutely forbid war. Why do the few rather than the many obtrude themselves into our minds? Why do we turn our eyes from Christ to men, and chuse rather to follow examples of doubtful authority, than an infallible guide, the Author and Finisher of our faith? The Roman pontiffs were but men; and it may have happened, that they were ill-advised, that they were inattentive, and lastly, that they were not overladen either with wisdom or piety.

Bernard, indeed, has praised warriors; but praised them in such a manner as to condemn, at the same time, the whole of our war system. But why should I care about the writings of Bernard, or the disputations of Thomas, when I have before my eyes the absolute prohibition of Christ, who, in plain terms, has told us, we must not resist evil; that is to say, not in the manner in which the generality of mankind do resist it, by violence and murder.

But they proceed to argue, that, as it is lawful to inflict punishment on an individual delinquent, it must also be lawful to take vengeance on an offending state. The full answer to be given to this argument would involve me in greater prolixity than is now requisite. I will only say, that the two cases differ widely in this respect: He who is convicted judicially, suffers the punishment which the laws impose; but in war, each side treats the other side as guilty, and proceeds to inflict punishment, regardless of law, judge, or jury. In the former case, the evil only falls on him who committed the wrong; the benefit of the example redounds to all: in the latter case, the greatest part of the very numerous evils falls on those who deserve no evil at all; on husbandmen, on old people, on mothers of families, on orphans, and on defenceless young females. But if any good at all can be gathered from a thing, (which is itself the worst of all things,) the whole of that good devolves to the share of a few most profligate robbers, to the mercenary pillager, to the piratical privateer, perhaps to a very few generals or statesmen, by whose intrigues the war was excited for this very purpose, and who never thrive so well as in the wreck of the Republic. In the former case, one man suffers for the sake of all; in the latter case, in order to revenge or serve the cause of a few, and, perhaps, of one man only, we cruelly afflict many thousand persons who gave no offence, and did no injury. It would be better to let the crime of a few go unpunished, than, while we endeavour to chastise one or two by war, in which, perhaps, we may not succeed, to involve our own people, the neighbouring people, and the innocent part of the enemies, for so I may call the multitude, in certain calamity. It is better to let a wound alone, which cannot be healed without injury to the whole body. But if any one should exclaim, 'that it would be unjust that he who has offended should not suffer condign punishment;' I answer, that it is much more unjust, that so many thousand innocent persons should be called to share the utmost extremity of misfortune which they could not possibly have deserved.

In these times, indeed, we see almost every war which breaks out, deriving its origin from some nugatory and obsolete pretence, or from the ambitious confederacies of princes, who, in order to bring some contested petty town under their jurisdiction, lead the whole empire into extreme jeopardy. After all, this petty town, or inconsiderable object, whatever it may be, claimed at the expense of much blood and treasure, is sold or ceded at the return of peace. Some one will say, would you not have princes prosecute their just rights? I am sensible that it is not the business of persons like me to dispute too freely upon the rights of princes, which, were it safe, would involve me in a longer discourse than would suit the present occasion. I will only say, that if every claim or disputable title be a sufficient cause for undertaking a war, that it is likely, in the multitudinous changes and chances of human affairs, a claim or disputable title will never be wanting for the purpose. What nation is there that has not been driven from some part of its territories, and which has not in its turn driven others? How often have men emigrated from one quarter to another? How often has the seat of empire been transferred hither and thither, either by chance, or by general consent? Now let the people of modern Padua, for instance, go and claim the territory of Troy, because Antenor, their founder, was a Trojan. Let the modern Romans put in their claim to Africa and Spain, because some of their provinces formerly belonged to the Romans of antiquity, their forefathers.

Add to this, that we are apt to call that dominion, or absolute property, which is only administration, or executive government on trust. There cannot be the same absolute right over men, all free by nature, as there is over cattle. This very right which you possess, limited as it is, was given you by the consent of the people. They who gave, unless I am mistaken, can take away. Now see how trifling a matter to the people is the subject in dispute. The point of contest is, not that this or that state may become subject to a good prince rather than to a bad one; but whether it should be given up as property to the claim of Ferdinand, or to the claim of Sigismund; whether it should pay tribute to Philip, or to Louis. This is that great and mighty right, for the establishment of which, the whole world is to be involved in one scene of war, confusion, and bloodshed.

But be it so; let this right be estimated as highly as you please; let there be no difference between the right to a man's private farm and to the public state; no difference between cattle bought with your own money, and men, not only born free, but become Christians; yet it would be the part of a wise man to weigh well in his mind, whether this right is of so much value as that he ought to prosecute it, at the expense of that immensity of calamities, which must be brought, by the prosecution of it, on his own people, on those who are placed under his tutelary care, and for whose good he wears the crown.

If, in forming this estimate, you cannot display the generosity of a truly princely character, yet at least shew us the shrewdness of a cunning tradesman, that knows and pursues his own interest. The tradesman despises a loss, if he sees it cannot be avoided without a greater loss; and sets it down as clear gain, if he can escape a dangerous risk at a trifling expense.

There is a trite little story that exhibits an example in private life, which it might not be amiss to follow, when the State is in danger of involving itself in war. There were two near relations, who could not agree on the division of some property which devolved to them; neither of them would yield to the other, and there seemed to be no possibility of avoiding a suit at law, and leaving the matter to be decided by the verdict of a jury. Counsel were retained, the process commenced, and the whole affair was in the hands of the lawyers. The cause was just on the point of being brought on, or, in other words, war was declared. At this period, one of the parties sent for his opponent, and addressed him to the following purpose: 'In the first place, said he, it is certainly unbecoming, (to speak in the most tender terms of it,) that two persons united like us by nature, should be dissevered by interest. In the second place, the event of a law-suit is no less uncertain than the event of war. To engage in it, indeed, is in our own power; to put an end to it is not so. Now the whole matter in dispute is one hundred pieces of gold. Twice that sum must be expended on notaries, on attornies, on counsellors, on the judges, and their friends, if we go to law about it. We must court, flatter, and fee them; not to mention the trouble of dancing attendance, and paying our most obsequious respects to them. In a word, there is more cost than worship in the business, more harm than good, and therefore I hope this consideration will weigh with you to give up all thoughts of a law-suit. Let us be wise for ourselves, rather than those plunderers; and the money that would be ill-bestowed on them, let us divide between ourselves. Do you give me one moiety from your share, and I will give you the same from mine. Thus we shall be clear gainers in point of love and friendship, which we should otherwise lose; and we shall escape all the trouble. But if you do not choose to yield any thing to me, why then, and in that case, I cheerfully resign the whole to you, and you shall do just as you please with it. I had rather the money should be in the hands of a friend, than in the clutches of those insatiable robbers. I shall have made profit enough by the bargain, if I shall have saved my character, kept my friend, and avoided the plague of a law-suit.'

The justice of these remarks, and the good humour with which they were made, overcame the adversary. They therefore settled the business between themselves.

In the infinitely more hazardous concerns of war, let statesmen condescend to imitate this instance of discretion. Let them not view merely the object which they wish to obtain, but how great a loss of good things, how many and great dangers, and what dreadful calamities they are sure of incurring, in trying to obtain it; and if they find, upon holding the scales with an even hand, and carefully weighing the advantages with the disadvantages, that peace, even with some circumstances of injustice, is better than a just war, why should they choose to risk the die of battle? Who, but a madman, would angle for a vile fish with a hook of gold? If they see much more loss than gain in balancing the account, even on the supposition that every thing happens fortunately, would it not be better to recede a little from their strict and rigorous right, than to purchase a little advantage at the high price of evils at once undefined and innumerable? Let the possessors keep their obsolete claims and titles unmolested, if I cannot dispute them without so great a loss of Christian blood.

But supposing Christians unable to despise, as they certainly ought, such trifles, yet why, on the breaking out of a dispute, must they rush instantly to arms? The world has so many grave and learned bishops, so many venerable churchmen of all ranks, so many grey headed grandees, whom long experience has rendered sage, so many councils, so many senates, certainly instituted by our ancestors for some useful purpose; why is not recourse had to their authority, and the childish quarrels of princes settled by their wise and decisive arbitration?

It is the part of a sensible man of the world to give these things due consideration; of a Christian, who is truly such, to shun, deprecate, and oppose, by every lawful means, a business so hellish, so irreconcileable both to the life and to the doctrine of Christ.

If we endeavour to be what we are called, that is, to be violently attached to nothing worldly, to seek nothing here with too anxious a solicitude; if we endeavour to free ourselves from all that may incumber and impede our flight to heaven; if we aspire with our most ardent wishes at celestial felicity; if we place our chief happiness in Christ alone, we have certainly, in so doing, made up our minds to believe, that whatever is truly good, truly great, truly delightful, is to be found in his religion. If we are convinced that a good man cannot be essentially hurt by any mortal; if we have duly estimated the vanity and transitory duration of all the ridiculous things which agitate human beings; if we have an adequate idea of the difficulty of transforming, as it were, a man into a god; of being so cleansed, by continual meditation, from the pollutions of this world, that when the body is laid down in the dust, one may emigrate to the society of angels: in a word, if we exhibit these three qualities, without which no man can deserve the appellation of a Christian; innocence, that we may be free from vice; charity, that we may deserve well of all men; patience, that we may bear with those who use us ill, and if possible, bury injuries by an accumulation of benefits on the injuring party; I ask what war can possibly arise hereafter for any trifles which the world contains?

If the Christian religion be a fable, why do we not honestly and openly explode it? Why do we glory and take a pride in its name? But if Christ is the way, and the truth, and the life, why do all our schemes of life and plans of conduct deviate so from this great exemplar? If we acknowledge Christ to be our Lord and Master, who is Love itself, and who taught nothing but love and peace, let us exhibit this model, not by assuming his name, or making an ostentatious display of the mere emblematic sign, his cross, but by our lives and conversation. Let us adopt the love of peace, that Christ may recognize his own, even as we recognise him to be the Teacher of pecae.

FINIS

OTTO DIX AND *DER KRIEG*

O T T O   D I X (1891-1969) *is an artist better known in his native Germany and Europe than in the United States, where his reputation has been overshadowed by his contemporaries, George Grosz, Max Beckmann, and other artists of the German Expressionist movement. Although Dix, throughout his long career, experimented with many styles—futurism, cubism, expressionism, even dadaism—and worked in all techniques—oil, pastel, watercolor and the various graphic media—he is most widely known as a satirical commentator on society. His sharply observed scenes of life during and after World War I in Germany and his probing and revealing portraits express a bold and bitter protest against the corruption and cynicism of his time, as well as a deep moral commitment to changing these conditions.*

In the early 1920's, Dix and other artists—among them Grosz, Schrimpf, and for a time Beckmann—founded the 'Neue Sachlichkeit' or 'New Objectivity' movement in reaction to the innumerable avant-gardist art trends, dadaist and expressionist primarily, which were swirling about in turbulent post-war Germany. This movement aimed to expose the reality of social evils by using the most meticulously realistic techniques. The result was, in Dix's work, an eerie kind of magic realism, an almost hallucinatory illumination of his subjects. The exaggerated and grotesque effect of these pictures was not accidental, but the outcome of the artist's intention to lay bare, in the most precise technique, a reality which was in itself distorted and grotesque. George Grosz's drawings and paintings of post-World-War I Germany, mocking and satirical though they are, always flicker with humor. Dix's, however, are more often infused with an almost savage intensity and seriousness, an attitude brought to its fullest expression in the fifty etchings which make up the cycle Der Krieg, *'The War.'*

Der Krieg, *published in Berlin in 1924, is justly considered to be a masterpiece of twentieth-century graphic art and one of the great and timeless statements against war by an artist of any age.*

The glorification and romanticization of war has always provided an opportunity for many artists to produce canvases bursting with picturesque battlefields, swashbuckling standard-bearers, and colorful heroes. Urs Graf, an artist contemporary with Erasmus, exemplified this attitude. For other artists the perception of the miseries, misfortunes and degradation that war brings to every aspect of human society has been a powerful impetus to the creation of works of art expressing, as did Erasmus, the opposite view of war.

Callot, Goya, Daumier, Kollwitz and Otto Dix have all produced great graphic statements on the disasters of war. It is interesting that each of these artists has chosen a series of prints as the vehicle for the expression of his ideas on war. It is as though only through the cumulative effect of a succession of powerful images, the building of one emotional scene upon another, could the full impact of the reality of war be expressed; no single image was capable of sustaining its weight. It is also significant that each of these artists chose the medium of the print from all others. One of the reasons, clearly, is the expressive possibilities inherent in the graphic techniques of etching, aquatint, lithography or woodcut, using subtly modulated or sharply contrasted blacks and whites. Moreover, prints are by their nature multiple—many impressions can be pulled from a single plate—so there is the possibility of communicating ideas to a wider audience.

Jacques Callot in 1633 etched two sets of plates, Les Grandes Misères de la Guerre, *consisting of eighteen large prints, and* Les Petites Misères de la Guerre, *six smaller etchings, which are a bitter portrayal of the disasters—burning, slaughter and rapine—visited upon the land and people of his native Lorraine during the Thirty Years' War. Though the compositions are extremely moving, the elegance and grace of Callot's etchings and the multiplicity of tiny images on these plates somewhat mitigate the harshness of their effect. Undoubtedly influenced by Callot's* Misères, *the Dutch artist Romeyn de Hooghe illustrated a book by Abraham de Wicquefort,* Advis Fidèle, *published in The Hague in 1673, with a series of vivid etchings showing violent scenes of French atrocities in the Netherlands. Daumier's great single statement on war, the ten plates gathered under the title L'Album du Siège in 1870-71, are infused with a sad and biting irony, and are often allegorical. Käthe Kollwitz's seven powerful woodcuts,* Der Krieg, *noble and monumental compositions which appeared shortly before Otto Dix's cycle in 1923, evoke a generalized sense of pity and sorrow at the suffering caused by war.*

Dix's Der Krieg, *however, invites comparison most closely with Goya's* Los Desastros de la Guerra. *Goya's series of eighty plates, etched in 1808, remained unpublished in his lifetime for fear of the political consequences; they were not struck until 1863. Dix chose to use etching and aquatint, the same medium Goya exploited so magnificently in all four of his great print series. Dix's prints also have, in common with Goya's, an immediacy and specificity of scene which produce a devastating effect of the unmitigated horror the artist felt in viewing these terrible events. Goya writes as a caption to one pitiful scene, 'Yo lo vi.'—'I saw this.' Dix, many years after Der Krieg was published, discussing the differences in the approach to the representation of war by the old masters and his own, remarked that the war pictures of the old masters looked as though the artist had never been there. Goya and Dix clearly were there. Goya saw these tragedies; Dix experienced them at first hand as a soldier in the trenches in the first World War.*

Otto Dix's Der Krieg *has a different scope from Goya's* Los Desastros. *Goya reveals, with vivid chiaroscuro, the tragedy that the madness of war has spread over Spain and all its people, in scene upon scene of cruelty and inhumanity. A number of the final plates indicate hope in the resurrection of Truth, after the nightmare is over and its reality has been perceived. Dix, in 1924, uses World War I as a microcosm of all wars. Most of the etchings deal directly with the horrors of trench warfare, some with the effects of war on the civilian population. A few, finally, show the moral corruption engendered by war: prostitutes and profiteers fatten on the general misery. Though the iconography includes gas masks, airplanes and shell-holes, specifics of modern warfare, the sense of desolation, destruction and demoralization apply to all wars, to war in general.*

World War I was a crucial experience for Dix and a watershed in the development of his art. Conscripted into the German army in 1914, he saw active service fighting in the trenches for four years and was wounded a number of times. In 1918 Dix returned to Dresden, and there he resumed his career as an artist.

Dresden, like all cities in defeated Germany, was experiencing the wretched aftermath of the war. Poverty, labor turmoil and rampant inflation created a pervasive demoralization and a disintegration of the social fabric. Yet even during these miserable and revolutionary post-war years, a flood of avant-garde creativity in the arts and in literature burst forth. Rejecting the grim past, collectors and connoisseurs preferred the newest in art to the old. Because the currency was inflated to the point of worthlessness, people chose to invest in art rather than to save money. From 1919 through the early 1920's, publishers and printers responded to the demand by producing magazines, books, journals and especially sumptuous portfolios of original graphic works by the leading contemporary artists, Beckmann, Grosz, Kokoschka, Barlach, Kandinsky and others. They found an eager and ready market.

During this period of post-war convulsion, with the memories of his wartime experiences yet to be exorcized, Dix drew and painted war subjects continuously, as, indeed, he had done throughout his army service. From 1920 to 1923 he worked on a great oil painting, Der Schützengraben, *'Trench Warfare,' one of his most important statements between the two world wars, a picture of such savage power that it evoked shocked outcries when it was shown. (It was later destroyed by the Nazis and is known today only in reproduction.) But the full expression of his thoughts on war was not to be achieved until he seized upon the idea of creating a cycle of prints, an idea for which the art of Callot, Goya, Daumier and Kollwitz provided the precedents.*

Dix chose as his medium etching with aquatint, rather than lithography, because the range of possibilities in this technique seemed richer and more expressive. After a period of intensive study to master these techniques completely, Dix set to work feverishly. In two great surges of creativity, in 1923 in Düsseldorf and early 1924 a Saig in the Black Forest, he produced the fifty etchings which make up Der Krieg. *An edition of seventy copies was printed by O. Felsing and published by Karl Nierendorf in Berlin in 1924. The fifty etchings, printed on Bütten paper under the artist's supervision, were laid into five cloth portfolios containing ten plates each. All the prints and the colophon are signed and numbered by Dix. It is impossible to say how many copies of the complete series were confiscated by the Nazis or destroyed in the Second World War. Of the surviving sets, a great many were taken apart and the etchings sold individually. Complete sets have, therefore, become quite rare; there cannot be more than a very small number in American collections today.*

Although, by the middle of 1924, the boom in the production and sale of the luxurious graphic volumes had begun to collapse, Dix's graphic masterpiece met with astonishing critical and commercial success. An inexpensive edition with photographic reproductions of twenty-four plates achieved a wide circulation.

Der Krieg *as a total work is truly astonishing in both the range of its expressiveness and its technical virtuosity. In these fifty plates every resource of the etching medium, from drypoint to the richest aquatint, is exploited to its fullest extent; even accidental effects are brilliantly incorporated. Each subject is treated in a technique appropriate to it. Night scenes have a special eeriness, the aquatint black and menacing with scenes of horror illuminated starkly:* Dance of Death, Anno'17 (Plate 19), Night Meeting with a Madman (Plate 22). *Others seem at first glance to be abstract compositions. A tracery of delicate white lines on a black background turns out to be, on closer view, a moonlit landscape pitted with shellholes (Plate 4). The best-known print of the series,* Stormtroops Advance under Gas *(Plate 12), is emblematic of dehumanization; the soldiers wearing gas-masks are transformed by their equipment into robot-like creatures. The violent composition,* A House Destroyed by Flying Bombs *(Plate 39), shows terrified women hanging from a house ripped apart in an air-raid. Simple, bold compositions in realistic style show the daily life in the trenches:* Transport of the Wounded at Houlthulster Forest *(Plate 47) or* Horse Cadaver *(Plate 5). Scenes of the corruption in the flesh markets of the home front are rendered in Dix's slashingly satiric style. A plate showing prostitutes on the street is entitled* Front Soldiers in Brussels *(Plate 34); their 'clients' are shown in another,* Sailors in Antwerp *(Plate 32).*

In the period between the two wars, with the rise of Nazism, Dix's work came under the censure of the government. He and most of the Expressionist artists were labeled Entartete, *'degenerates' whose work was not allowed to be shown, and whose paintings were often destroyed. His 'degeneracy' as an artist, however, did not prevent his being drafted into the German army in 1943. Captured quite soon, he spent the rest of the war in a French prisoner-of-war camp near Colmar.*

Dix died in 1969 at the age of seventy-seven, honored in Germany by innumerable awards, exhibitions and publications in the last years of his life—fitting recognition on the part of his country of a gifted artist of great integrity whose contribution to twentieth-century German art would have been considerable had he created only Der Krieg.

CHARLOTTE Z. VERSHBOW

LIST OF ETCHINGS

—

FACSIMILE OF *DER KRIEG*
BY OTTO DIX

I

2. VERSCHÜTTETE (JANUAR 1916, CHAMPAGNE)
Buried (January 1916, Champagne)

3. GASTOTE (TEMPLEUX-LA-FOSSE, AUGUST 1916)
Killed By Gas (Templeux-La-Fosse, August 1916)

4. TRICHTERFELD BEI DONTRIEN VON LEUCHTKUGELN ERHELLT
Crater-Field at Dontreix Lit by Fire Bombs

6. VERWUNDETER (HERBST 1916, BAPAUME)
Wounded Man (Fall 1916, Bapaume)

7. BEI LANGEMARK (FEBRUAR 1918)
At Langemark (February 1918)

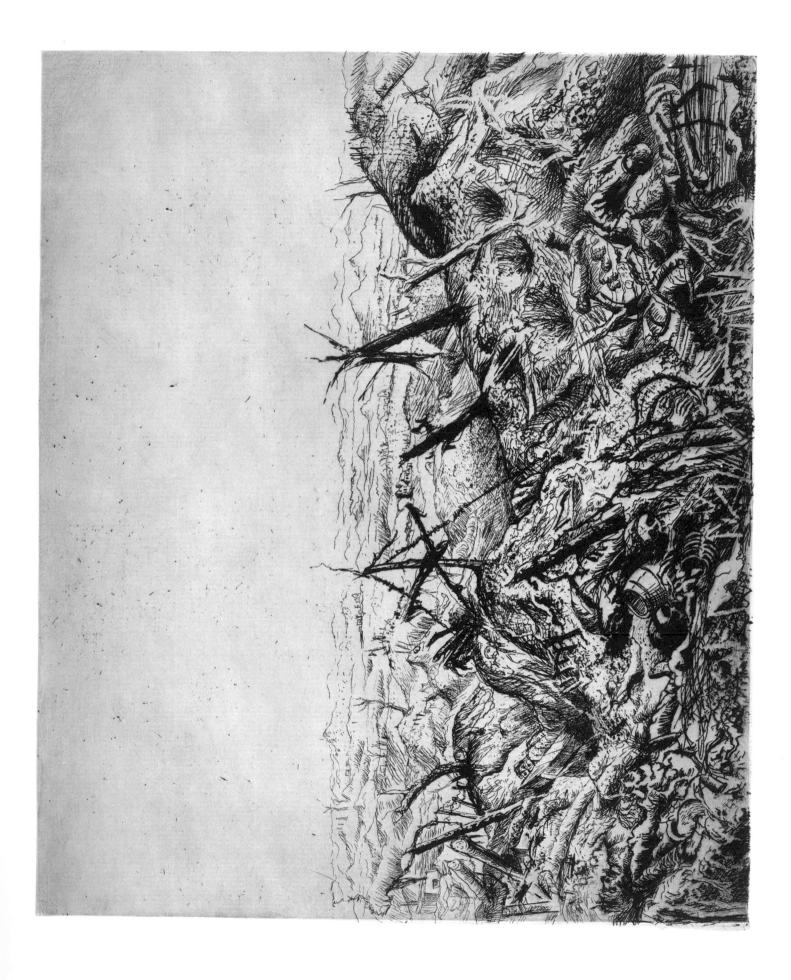

8. RELAISPOSTEN (HERBSTSCHLACT IN DER CHAMPAGNE)
Relay Post (Autumn Battle in Champagne)

9. ZERFALLENDER KAMPFGRABEN
Ruined Battletrench

10. FLIEHENDER VERWUNDETER (SOMMESCHLACT 1916)
Wounded Man Fleeing (Somme Battle 1916)

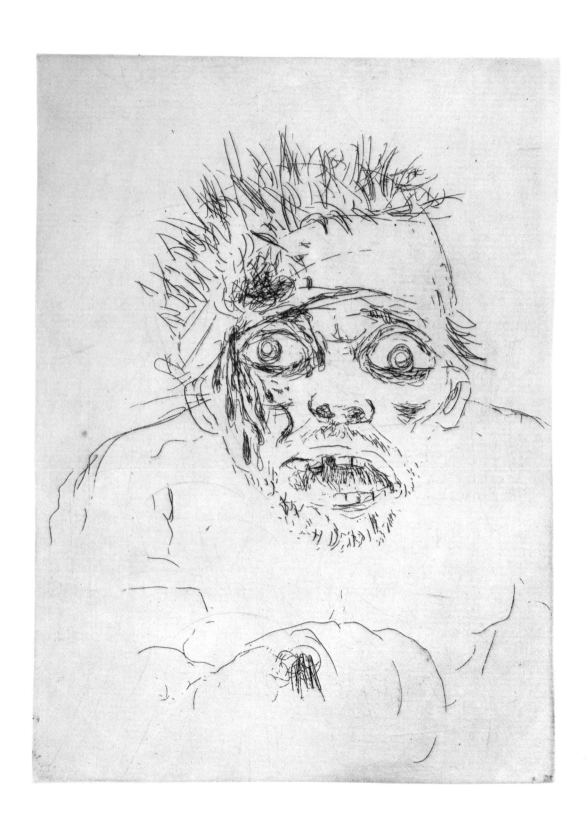

II

II. VERLASSENE STELLUNG BEI NEUVILLE
Abandoned Battlestation at Neuville

12. STURMTRUPPE GEHT UNTER GAS VOR
Stormtroops Advance Under Gas

13. MAHLZEIT IN DER SAPPE (LORETTO HÖHE)
Mealtime in the Trenches (Loretto Heights)

19. TOTENTANZ ANNO 17 (HÖHE TOTER MANN)
Dance of Death, Anno 17 (Upraised Dead Man)

20. DIE II. KOMPAGNIE WIRD HEUTE NACHT ABGELÖST
Company II will be Relieved Tonight

III

21. ABGEKÄMPFTE TRUPPE GEHT ZURÜCK (SOMMESCHLACHT)
Battleweary Troops Return (Somme Battle)

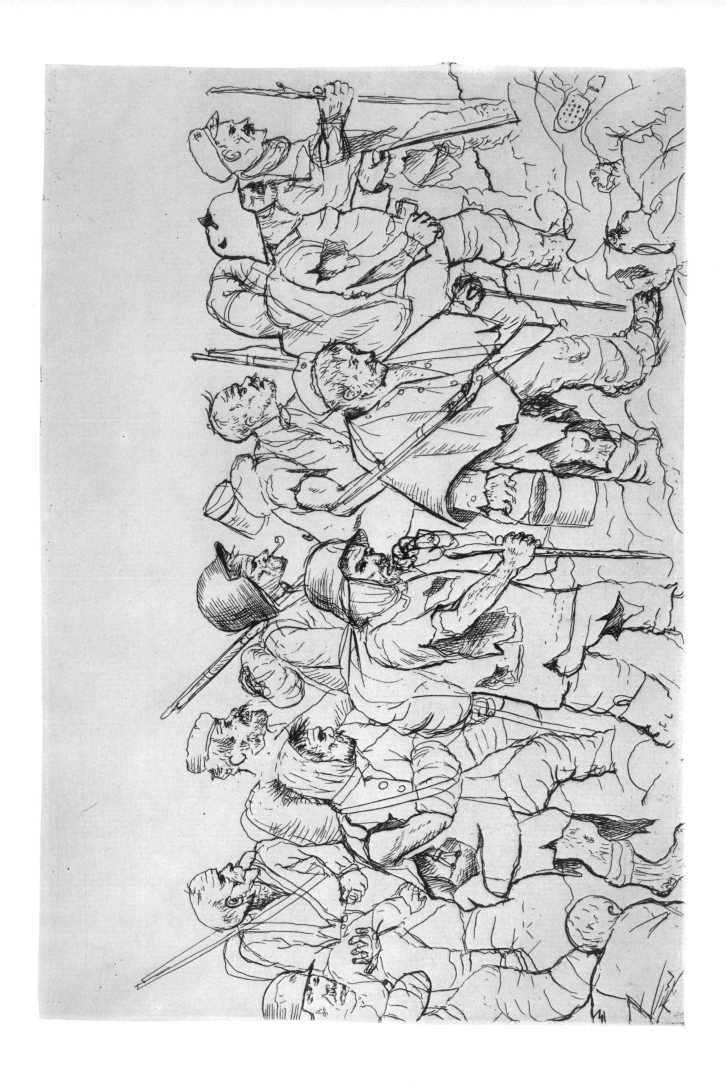

22. NACHTLICHE BEGEGNUNG MIT EINEM IRRSINNIGEN
Night Meeting with a Madman

23. TOTER IM SCHLAMM
Dead Man in the Mud

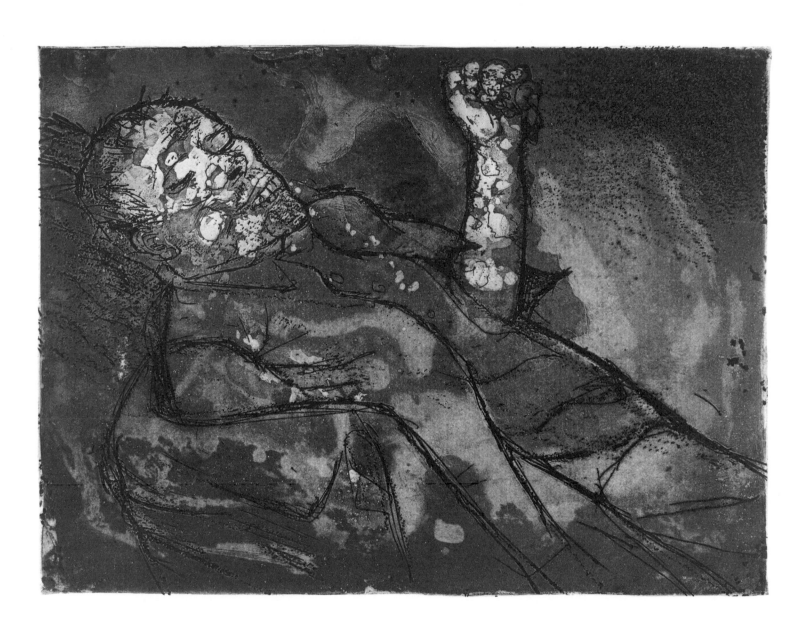

24. GRANATTRICHTER MIT BLUMEN (FRÜHLING 1916 VOR REIMS)
Shell Crater with Flowers (Spring 1916, Before Reims)

26. STERBENDER SOLDAT
Dying Soldier

27. ABEND IN DER WIJTSCHAETE-EBENE (NOVEMBER 1917)
Evening in Wijtschaete Plain (November 1917)

28. GESEHEN AM STEILHANG VON CLERY-SUR-SOMME
Seen on the Heights of Clery-Sur-Somme

30. DRAHTVERHAU VOR DEM KAMPFGRABEN
Wire Entanglement in Front of a Battle Trench

IV

31. SCHÄDEL
Skull

34. FRONTSOLDAT IN BRÜSSEL
Front Soldiers in Brussels

35. DIE IRRSINNIGE VON ST. MARIE-À-PY
The Madwoman of St. Marie-à-Py

36. BESUCH BEI MADAME GERMAINE IN MÉRICOURT
A Visit to Madame Germaine in Méricourt

37. KANTINE IN HAPLINCOURT
Canteen at Haplincourt

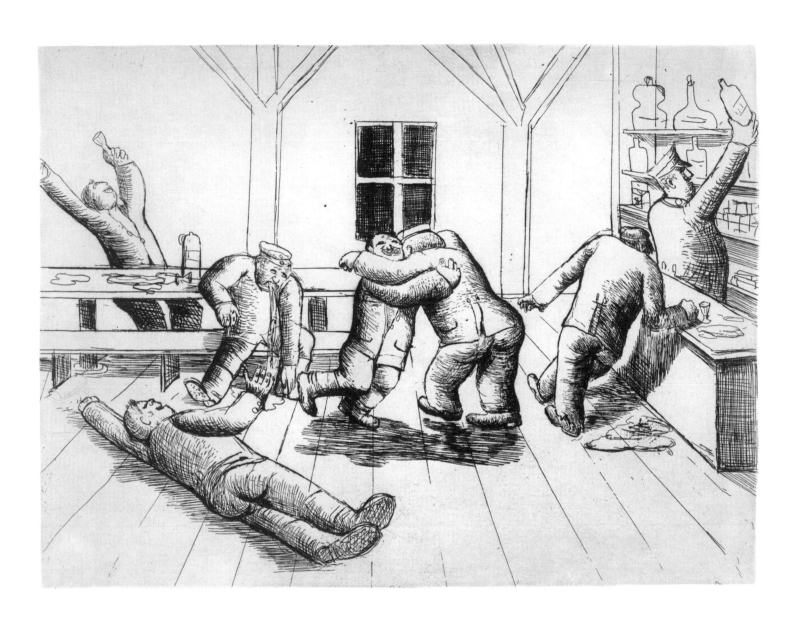

38. ZERSCHOSSENE
Shot to Pieces

39. DURCH FLIEGERBOMBEN ZERSTRTÖES HAUS (TOURNAI)
A House Destroyed by Flying Bombs (Tournai)

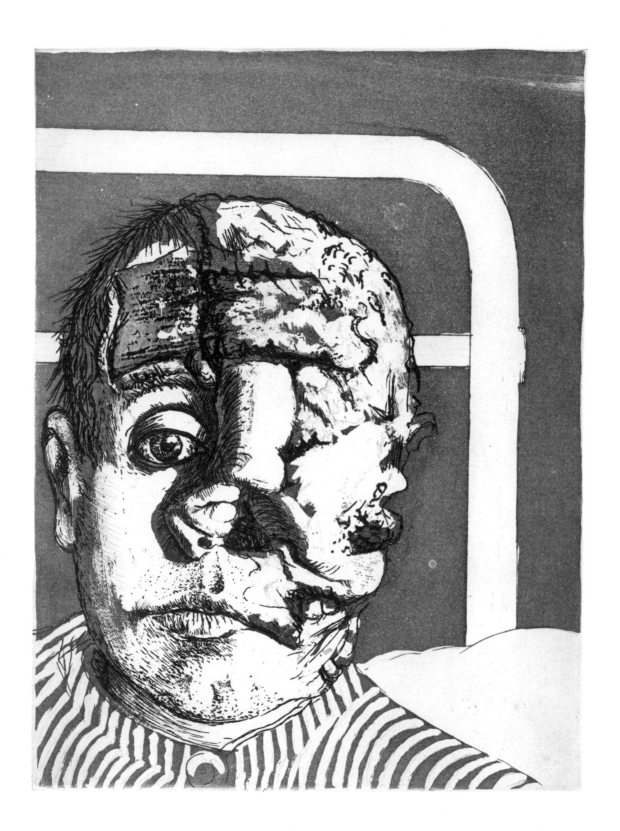

V

42. TOTER (ST. CLÉMENT)
Dead Man (St. Clément)

43. ESSENHOLEN BEI PILKEM
Getting Dinner at Pilken

44. ÜBERFALL EINER SCHLEICHPATROUILLE AUF EINEN GRABENPOSTEN
Surprise Attack on a Trench Sentry by a Prowling Patrol

45. UNTERSTAND
Dugout

46. DIE SCHLAFENDEN VOM FORT VAUX (GAS-TOTE)
The Sleepers of Fort Vaux (Killed by Gas)

47. VERWUNDETENTRANSPORT IM HOULTHULSTER WALD
Transport of the Wounded at Houlthulster Forest

48. DIE SAPPENPOSTEN HABEN NACHTS DAS FEUER ZU UNTERHALTEN
The Trench Sentries Have to Keep up the Firing at Night

49. APPELL DER ZURÜCKGEKEHRTEN
Roll Call of the Ones who Came Back

50. TOTE VOR DER STELLUNG BEI TAHURE
Dead at Their Station in Tahure

This edition of nineteen hundred and fifty numbered copies has been designed and printed at the press of David R. Godine in Brookline, Massachusetts. The text is set in Monotype Spectrum by Mackenzie and Harris, Inc., and printed on Monadnock Laid. The etchings by Otto Dix from Arthur & Charlotte Vershbow's intact original portfolio of Der Krieg are reproduced by The Meriden Gravure Company, Connecticut. The binding is by New Hampshire Bindery.

This is copy number

092092

092092